THE BEST OF

THE SMITHS

© Lawrence Watson / Retna

ISBN 978-1-4234-9264-1

HAL•LEONARD®
CORPORATION
7777 W. BLUEMOUND RD. P.O. BOX 13819 MILWAUKEE, WI 53213

CONTENTS

BIGMOUTH STRIKES AGAIN

Words and Music by JOHNNY MARR
and STEVEN MORRISSEY

Energetically

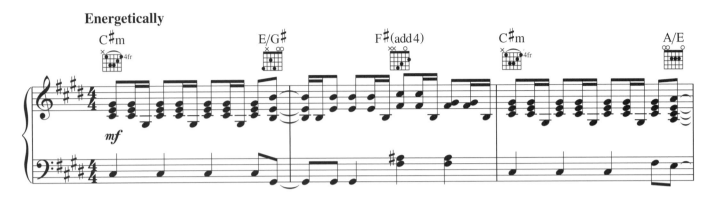

Sweet - ness, sweet - ness, I____ was on - ly

jok - ing when I said____ I'd like____ to smash ev - 'ry tooth in____

your head.____

Oh,____

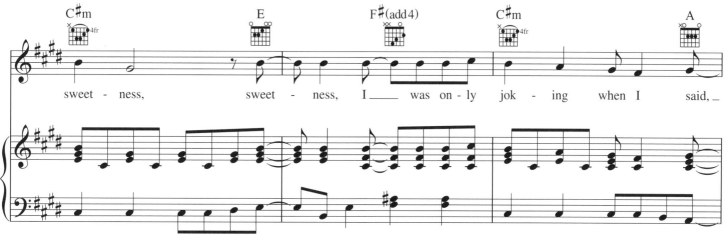

sweet - ness, sweet - ness, I ____ was on - ly jok - ing when I said, __

____ by rights, __ you should be bludg - eoned in ____ your bed.

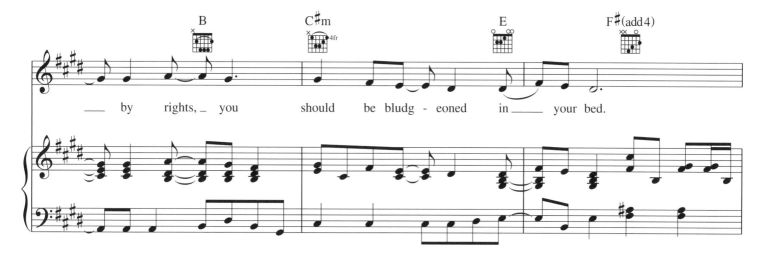

And now I know how Joan of Arc felt, now __

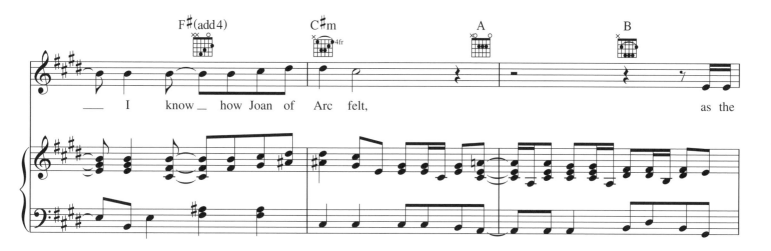

____ I know __ how Joan of Arc felt, as the

flames rose _____ to her Rom-an nose and her {Walk-man / hear-ing aid} start-ed _____ to melt. _____

Ooh. _____

Ooh, ooh, _____

ooh. _____

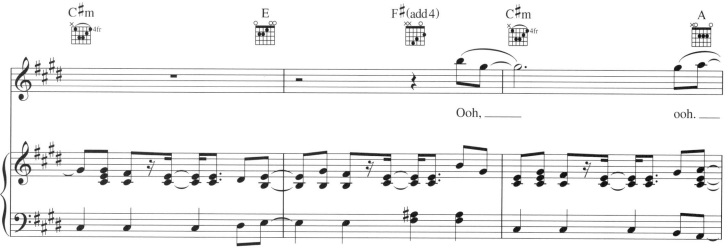

Ooh, _____ ooh. _____

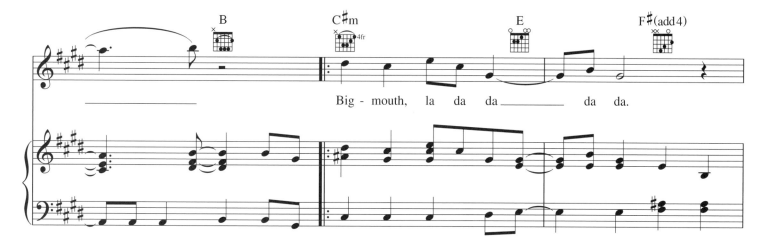

_____ Big - mouth, la da da _____ da da.

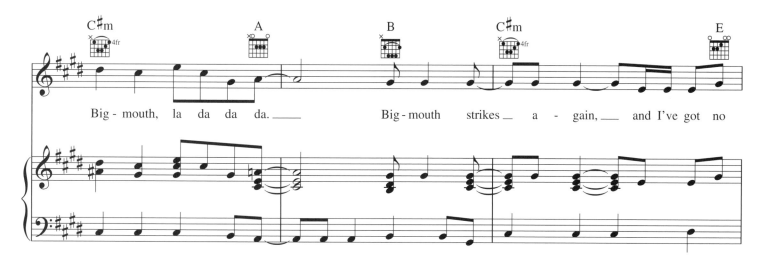

Big - mouth, la da da da. _____ Big - mouth strikes _____ a - gain, _____ and I've got no

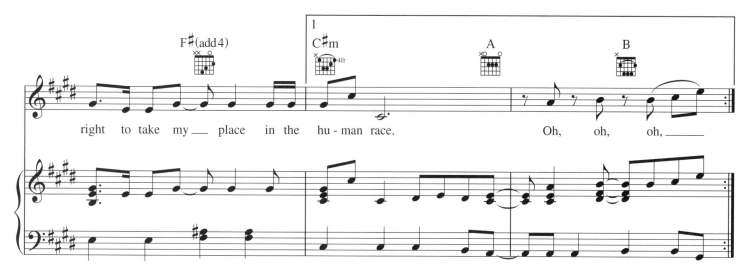

right to take my _____ place in the hu - man race. Oh, oh, oh, ____

hu - man race.

And now I know how Joan of

D.S. al Coda

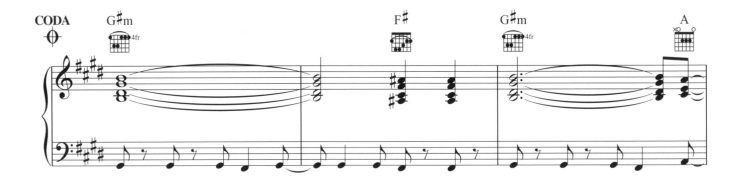

CODA

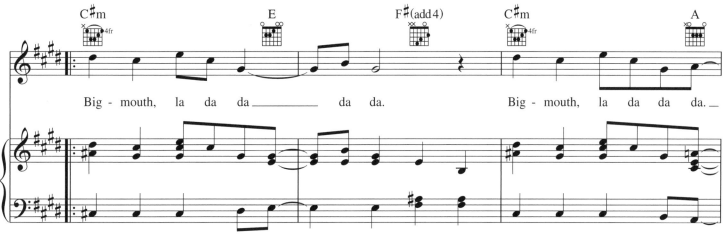

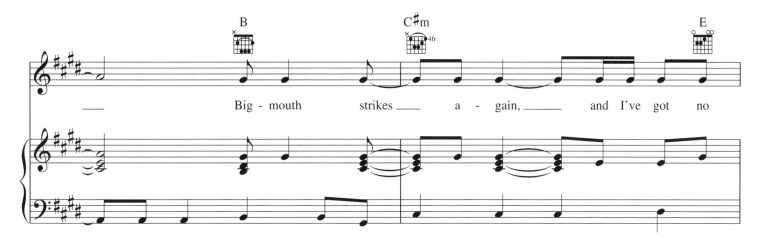

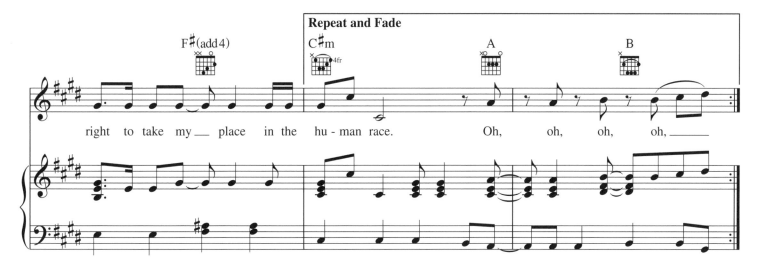

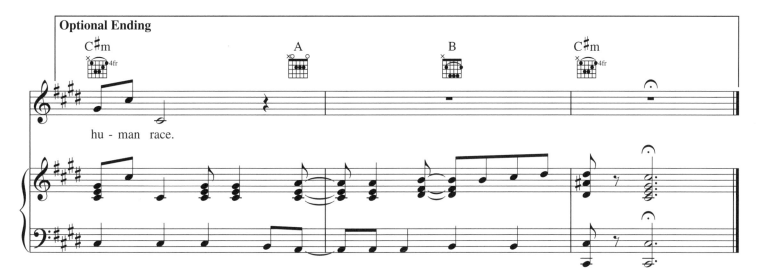

THE BOY WITH THE THORN IN HIS SIDE

Words and Music by JOHNNY MARR
and STEVEN MORRISSEY

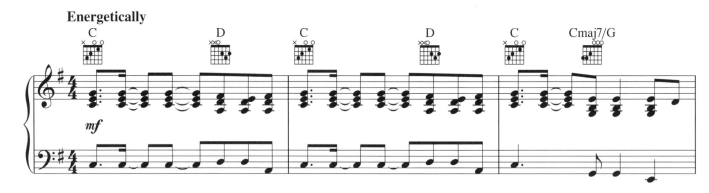

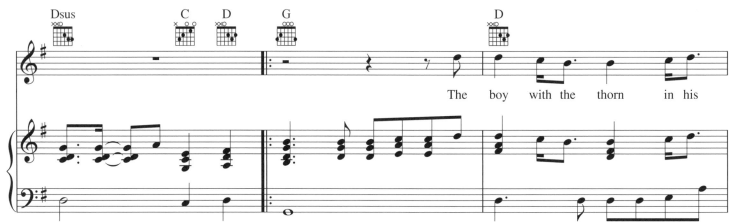

The boy with the thorn in his

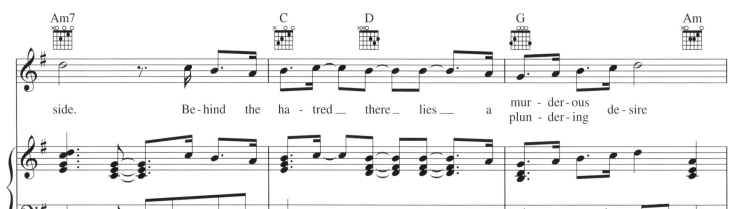

side. Be-hind the ha-tred __ there __ lies __ a mur-der-ous
plun-der-ing de-sire

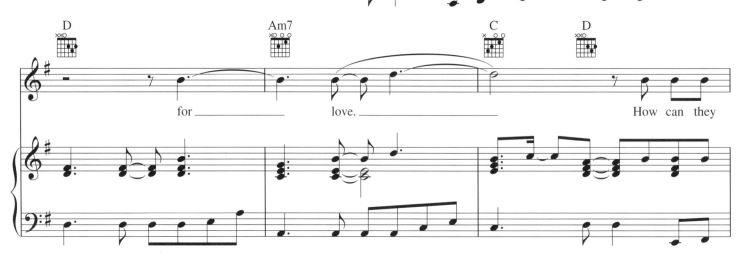

for _____ love. _____ How can they

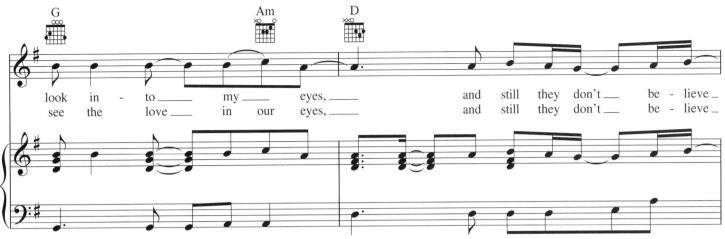

look in - to _____ my _____ eyes, _____ and still they don't ___ be - lieve _____
see the love _____ in our eyes, _____ and still they don't ___ be - lieve _____

___ me? _____ How can they hear me say ___ those ___ words, _
___ us? _____ And af - ter all this time,

_____ still _____ they don't ___ be - lieve _____ me? _____
they don't want to be - lieve _____ us? _____

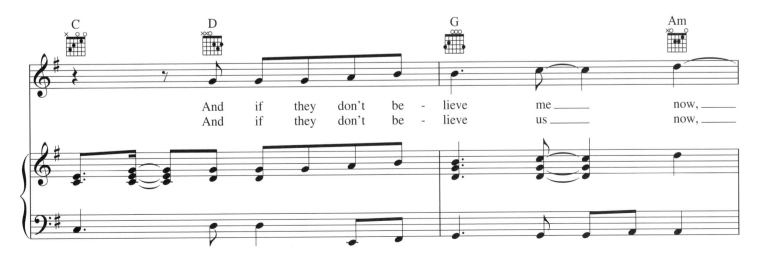

And if they don't be - lieve me _____ now, _____
And if they don't be - lieve us _____ now, _____

12

will they ev-er _____ be-lieve me? _____ And if they don't be-
will they ev-er _____ be-lieve us? _____ And when you want to

lieve me _____ now, _____ will they ev-, will they ev - er _____
live, how do you start? Where do you go? Who do you _____ need _____

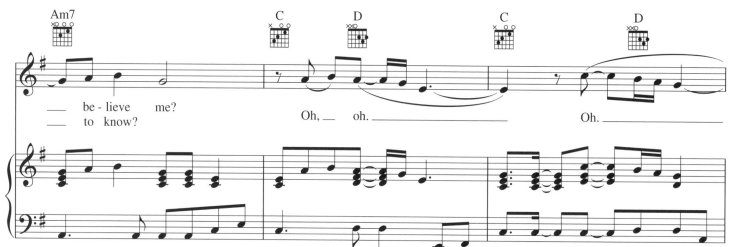

_____ be-lieve me?
_____ to know? Oh, __ oh. _____ Oh. _____

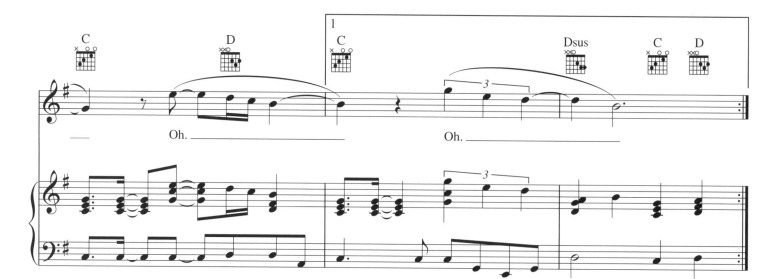

Oh. _____ Oh. _____

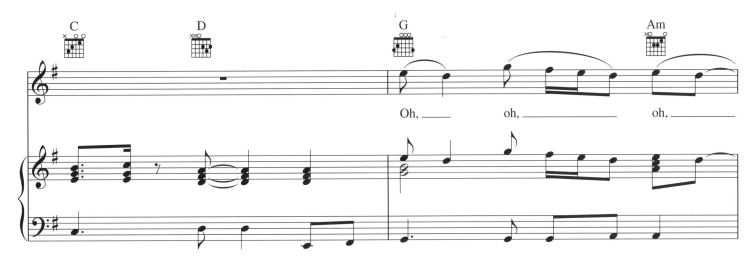

No, _____ no, no, no. _____ No, __ no, no, no. _____ No, no, _
Vocal ad lib. on repeats

__ no, _____ no, _____ no. _____ No, no, __ no, no, no, no, _____ no, no,

Play 4 times

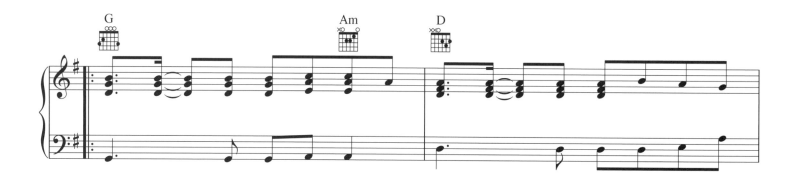

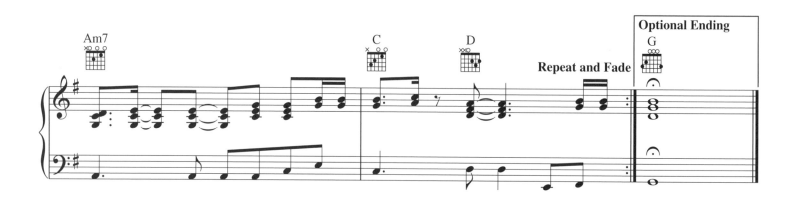

Repeat and Fade

Optional Ending

HAND IN GLOVE

Words and Music by JOHNNY MARR
and STEVEN MORRISSEY

Bright Rock

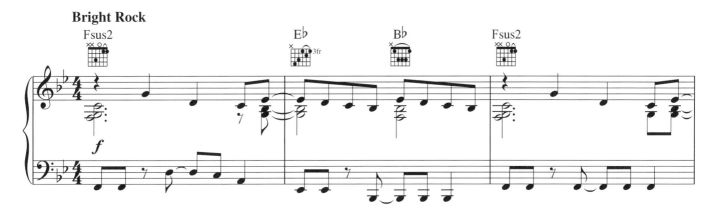

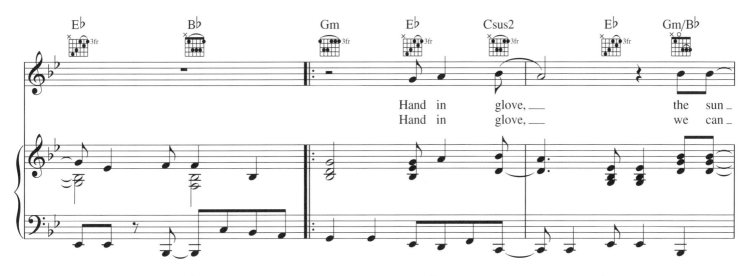

Hand in glove, ___ the sun
Hand in glove, ___ we can

___ shines out ___ of our be - hinds. ___ No, it's not like an - y oth - er love. ___
___ go wher - ev - er we please. And ev - 'ry - thing de - pends ___

This one is diff-'rent be-cause it's us. _____
up - on ____ how close you stand to me. _____

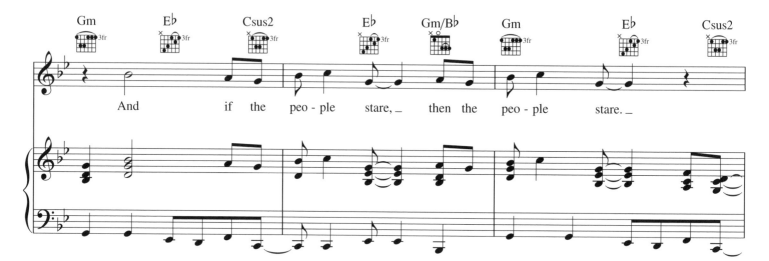

And if the peo - ple stare, _ then the peo - ple stare. _

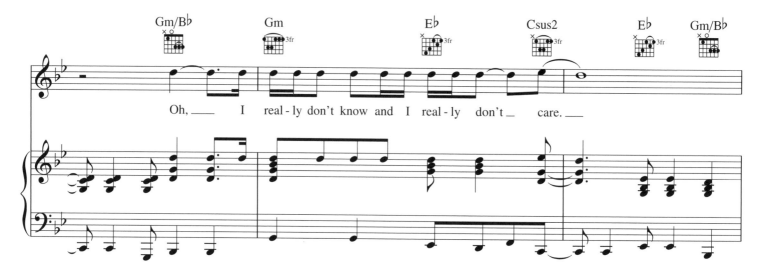

Oh, ____ I real - ly don't know and I real - ly don't _ care. ____

Lose _____ my share. _____ Ooh, _

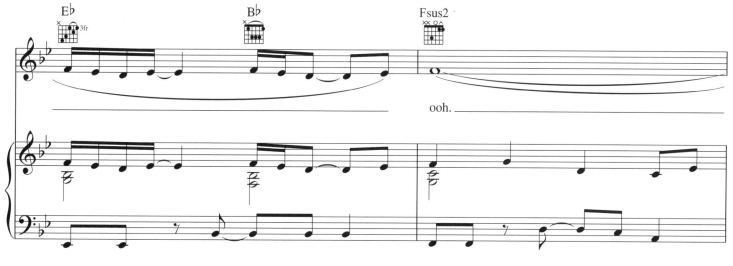

ooh.

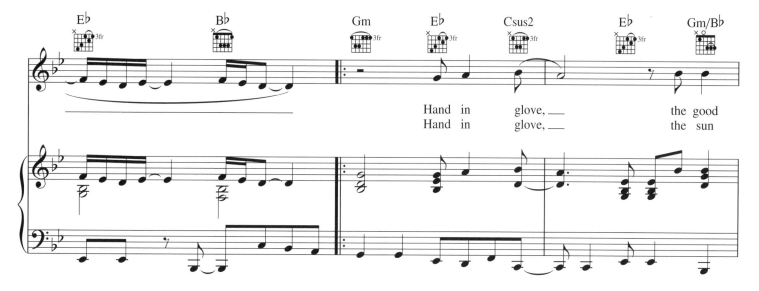

Hand in glove, ___ the good
Hand in glove, ___ the sun

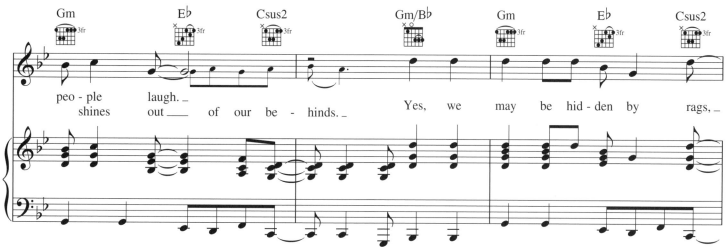

peo - ple laugh. _ Yes, we may be hid - den by
shines out ___ of our be - hinds. _ Yes, we may be hid - den by rags, _

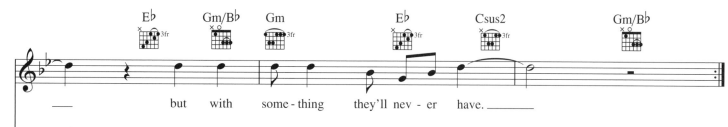

___ but with some - thing they'll nev - er have. _____

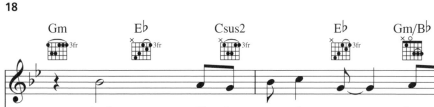

And if the peo-ple stare, _ then the peo-ple stare. _

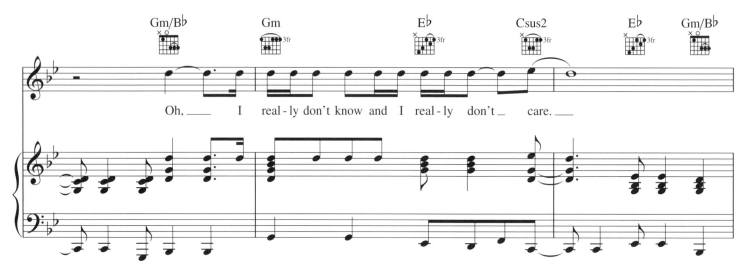

Oh, ___ I real-ly don't know and I real-ly don't _ care. ___

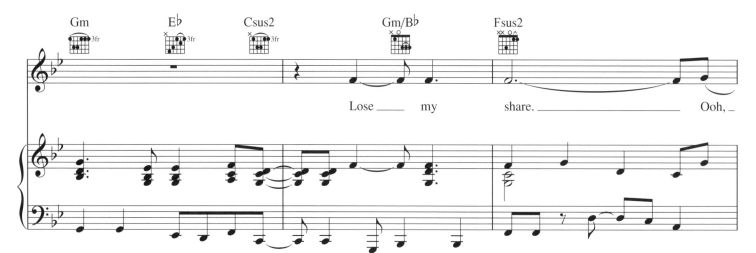

Lose ___ my share. _____ Ooh, _

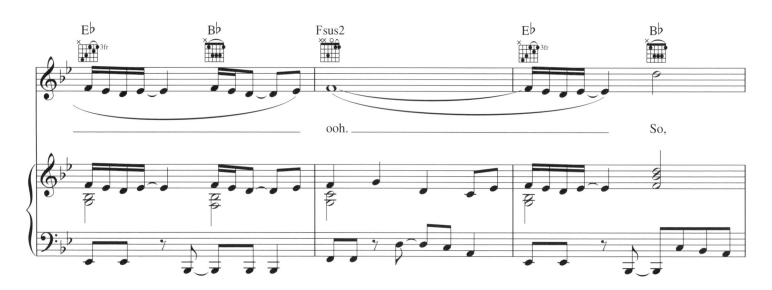

_____ ooh. _____ So,

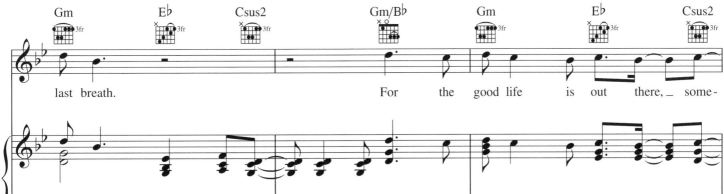

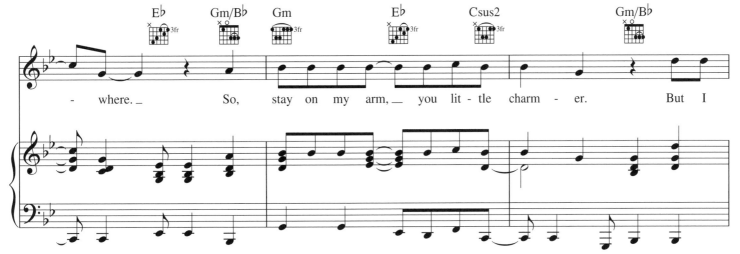

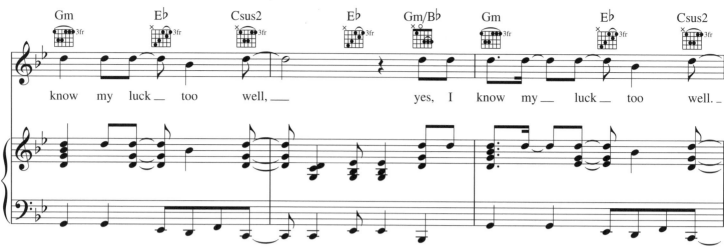

know my luck __ too well, ___ yes, I know my __ luck __ too well. __

___ And I'll prob-'ly nev-er see you a-gain. ___ I'll

prob-'ly nev-er see you a-gain. ___ I'll prob-'ly nev-er

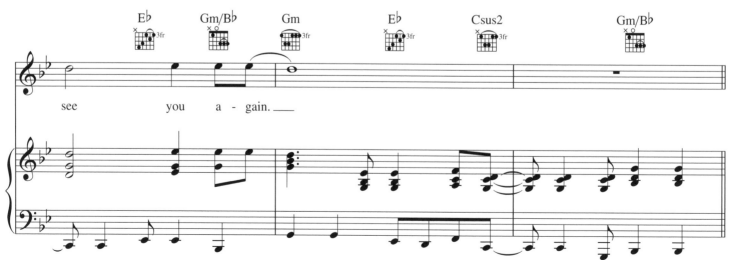

see you a-gain. ___

Ooh, _____ ooh, _____ ooh. _____

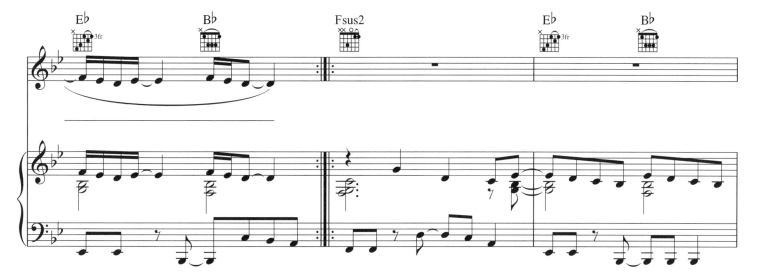

Repeat and Fade | Optional Ending

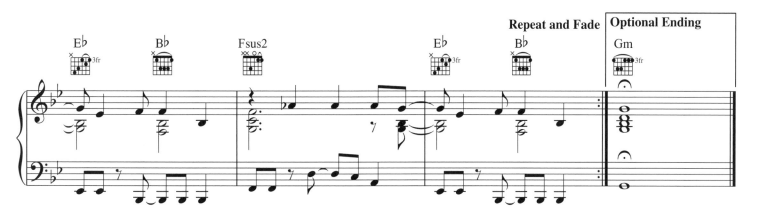

GIRLFRIEND IN A COMA

Words and Music by JOHNNY MARR
and STEVEN MORRISSEY

Relaxed Pop

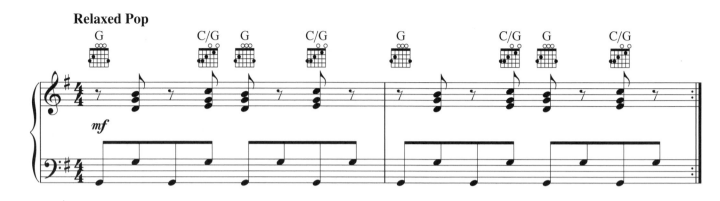

Girl-friend in a co-ma, I know, I know it's se-ri-ous.

Girl-friend in a co-ma, I know, I know it's real-ly

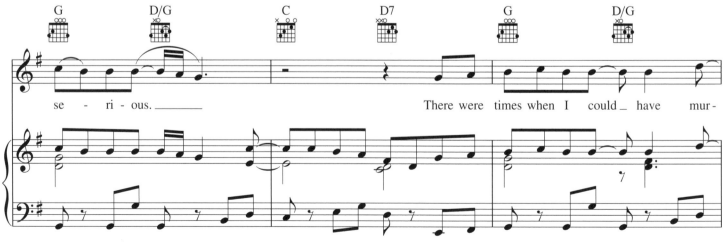

se-ri-ous. There were times when I could have mur-

-dered_ her. ___ But you know, I would hate an-y-thing to

hap-pen to her. _____ No, I don't want to see her. Do you

real-ly think she'll pull through? Do you real-ly think she'll_ pull through?_

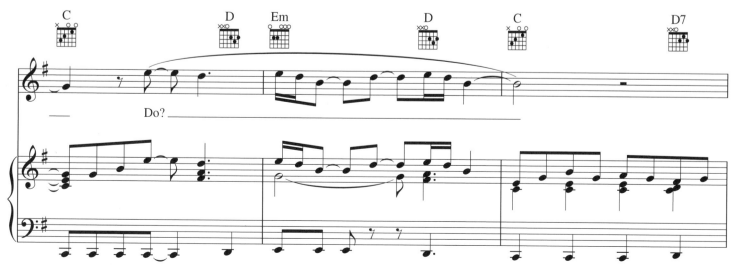

__ Do? _____

Girl-friend in a co-ma, I know,_ I know_ it's se - ri - ous._

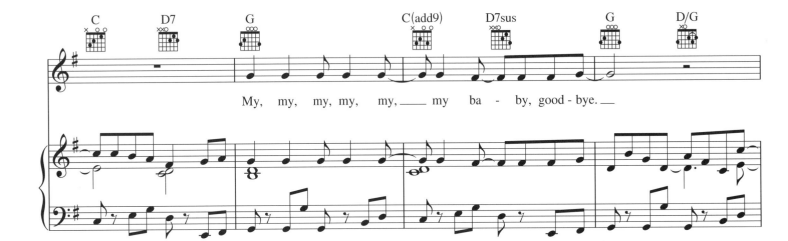

My, my, my, my, my,_ my ba - by, good - bye._

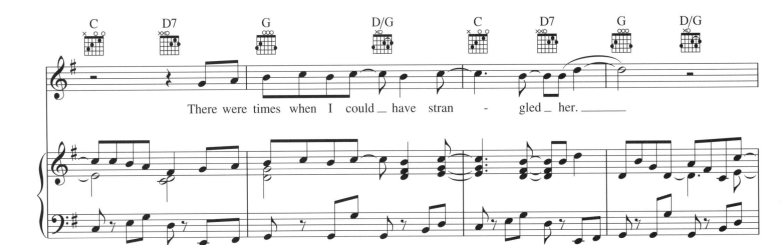

There were times when I could_ have stran - gled_ her._

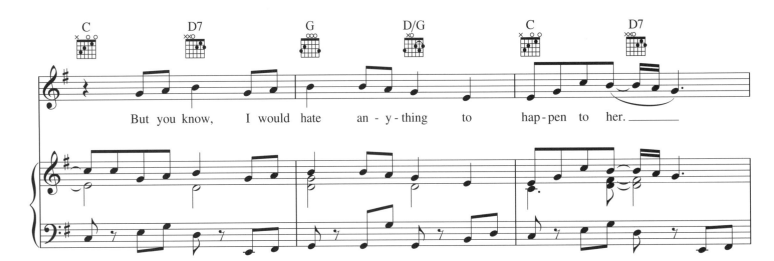

But you know, I would hate an - y - thing to hap - pen to her._

Would you please __ let me see her? Do you real - ly think __ she'll pull

through? Do you real - ly think she'll __ pull through? __ Do? _____

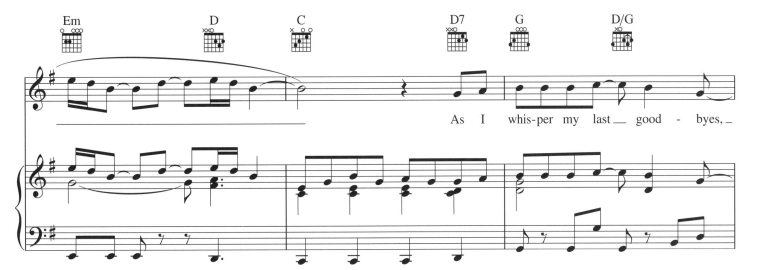

As I whis-per my last __ good - byes, __

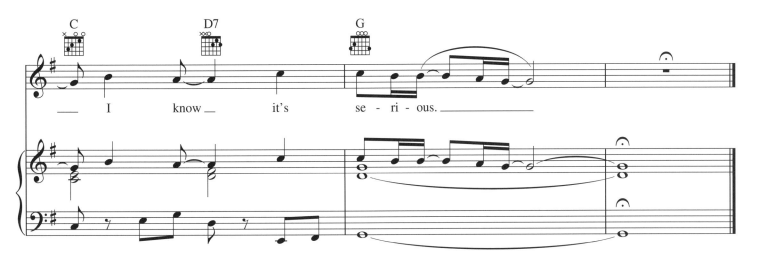

__ I know __ it's se - ri - ous. _____

THE HAND THAT ROCKS THE CRADLE

Words and Music by JOHNNY MARR
and STEVEN MORRISSEY

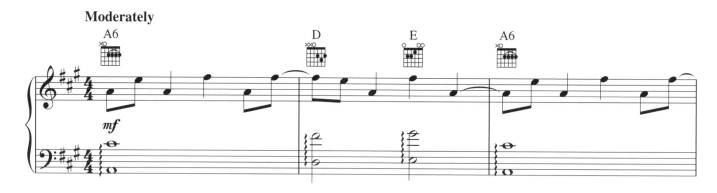

Moderately

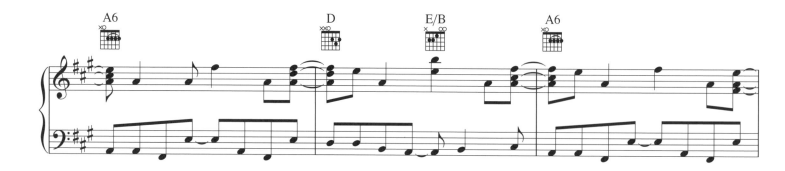

Please don't cry, _

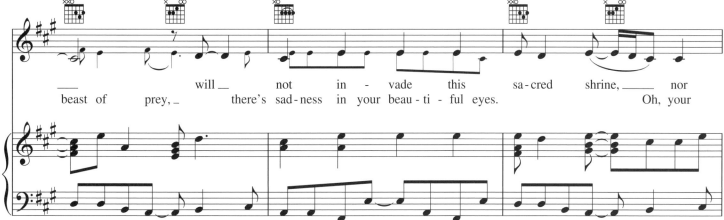

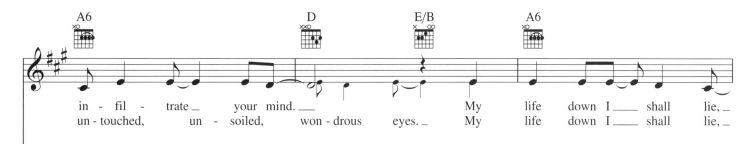

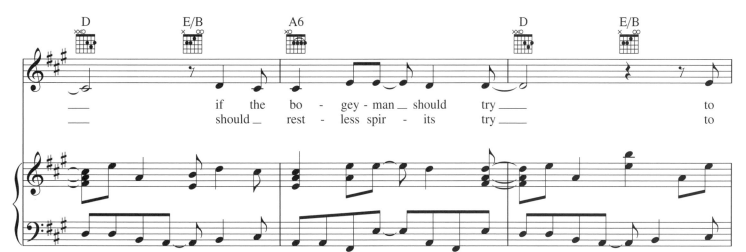

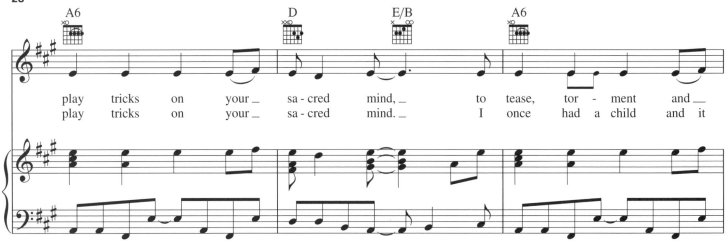

play tricks on your __ sa-cred mind, __ to tease, tor - ment and __
play tricks on your __ sa-cred mind. __ I once had a child and it

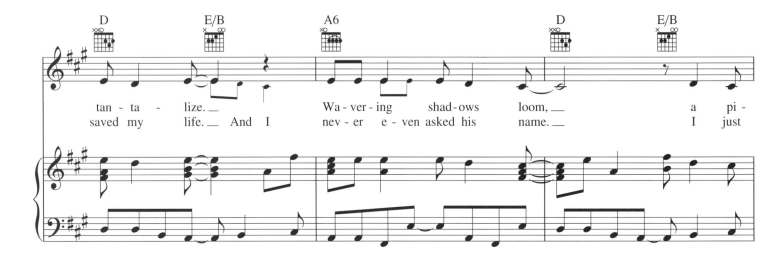

tan - ta - lize. __ Wa-ver-ing shad-ows loom, __ a pi-
saved my life. __ And I nev-er e-ven asked his name. __ I just

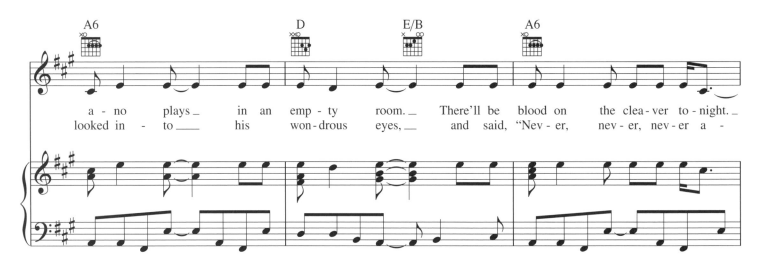

a - no plays __ in an emp-ty room. __ There'll be blood on the clea-ver to-night. __
looked in - to __ his won-drous eyes, __ and said, "Nev-er, nev-er, nev-er a-

__ And when dark - ness lifts and the room is bright, __ I'll
gain." And all too soon I did-n't re - turn

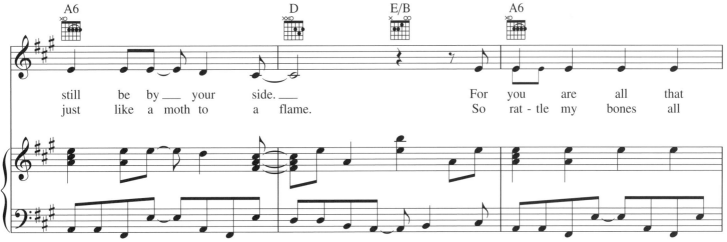

still be by ___ your side. ___ For you are all that
just like a moth to a flame. So rat-tle my bones all

mat - ters, and ___ I'll love you 'til the day I die. ___ There
o - ver the stones, I'm on - ly a beg-gar-man who no-bod-y owns. ___ I'll

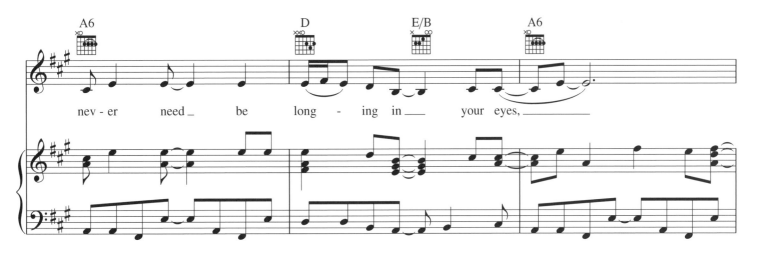

nev - er need ___ be long - ing in ___ your eyes, ___

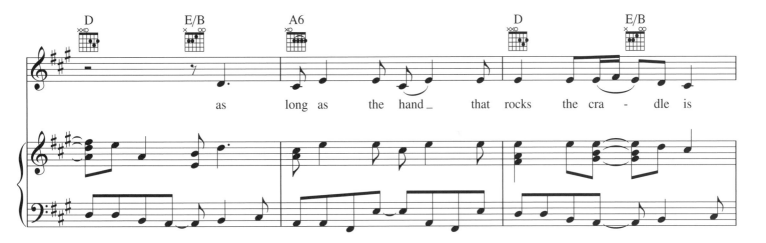

as long as the hand ___ that rocks the cra - dle is

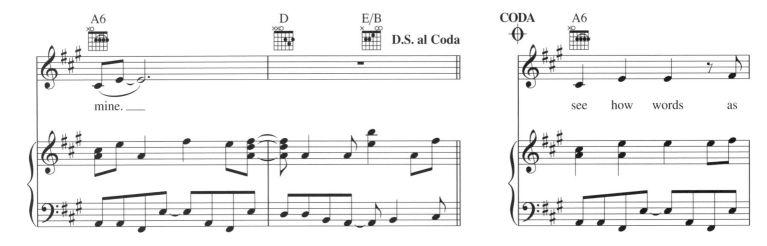

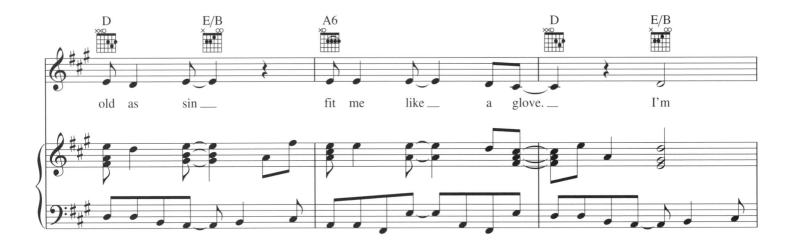

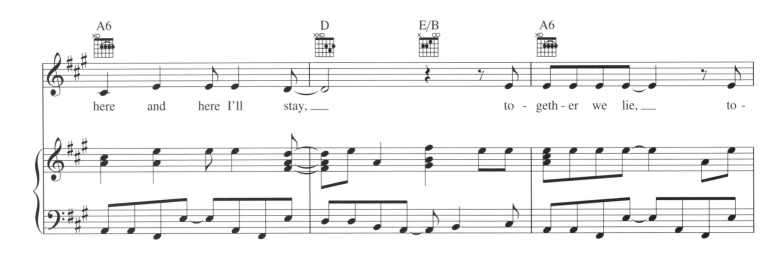

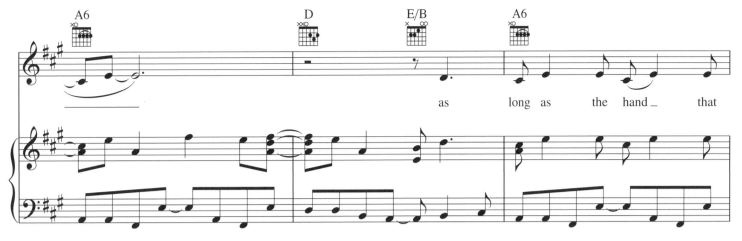

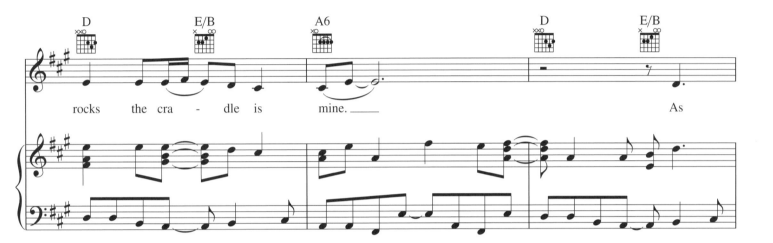

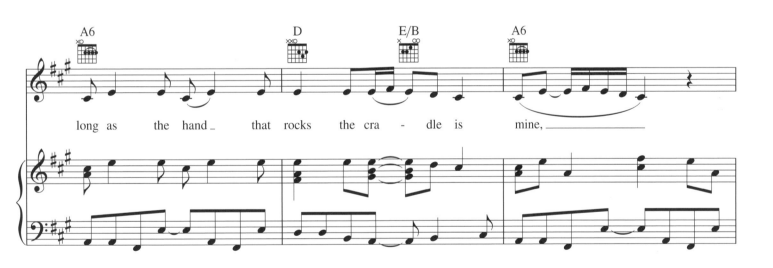

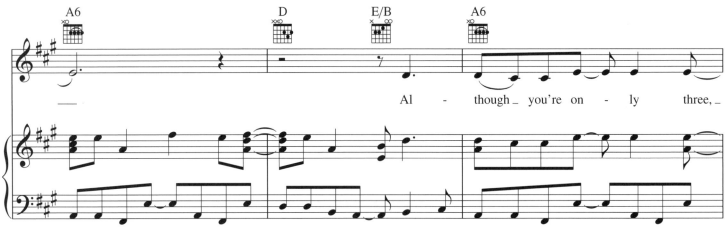

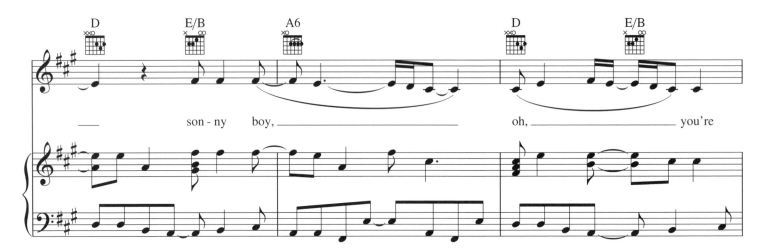

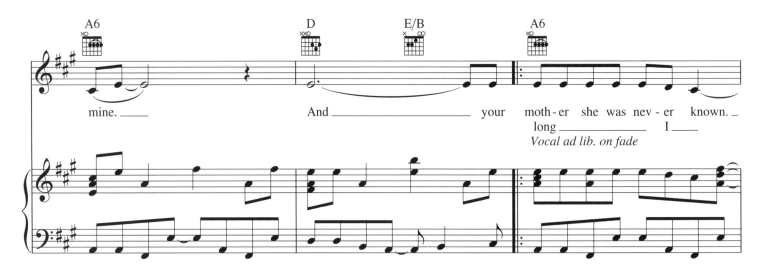

HEAVEN KNOWS I'M MISERABLE NOW

Words and Music by JOHNNY MARR
and STEVEN MORRISSEY

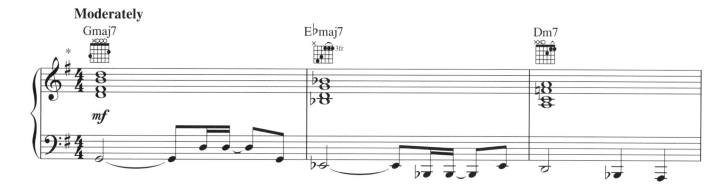

I was hap-py in the haze of a

asked of ___ me at the

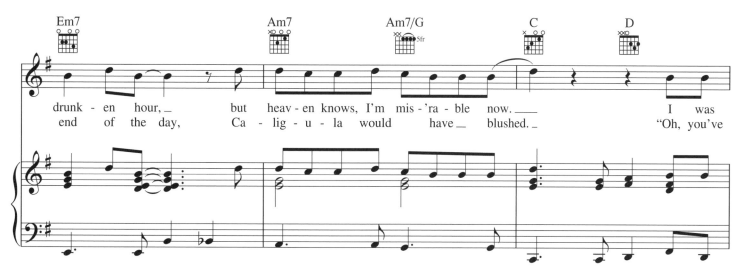

drunk-en hour, ___ but heav-en knows, I'm mis-'ra-ble now. ___ I was

end of the day, Ca-lig-u-la would have ___ blushed. ___ "Oh, you've

Recorded a half step lower.

34

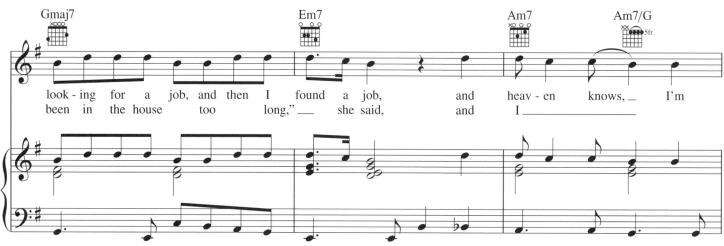

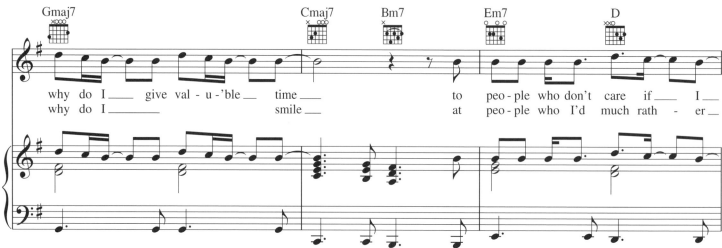

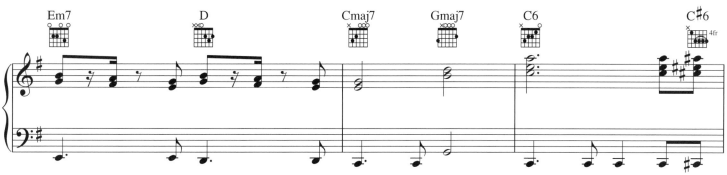

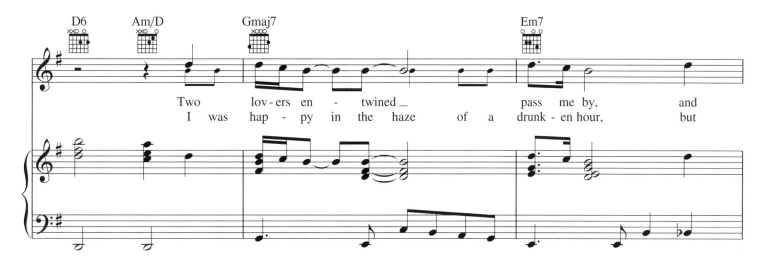

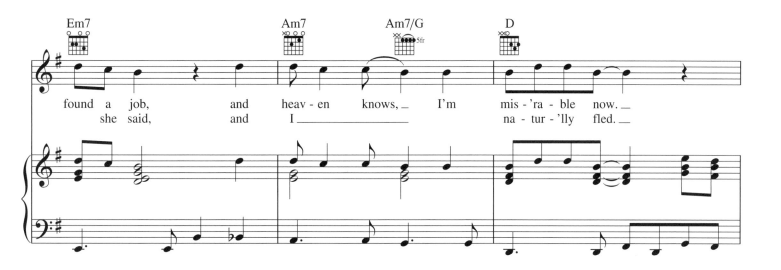

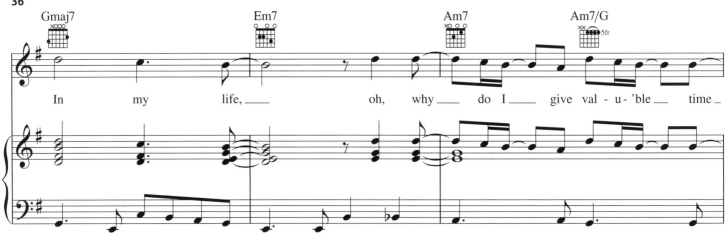

In my life, ___ oh, why ___ do I ___ give val - u - 'ble ___ time ___

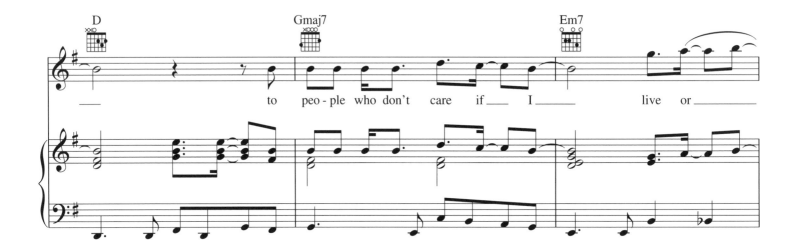

___ to peo - ple who don't care if ___ I ___ live or ___

___ die? _

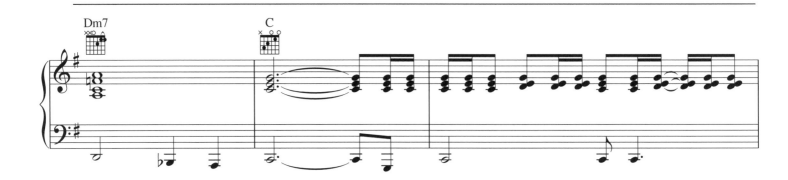

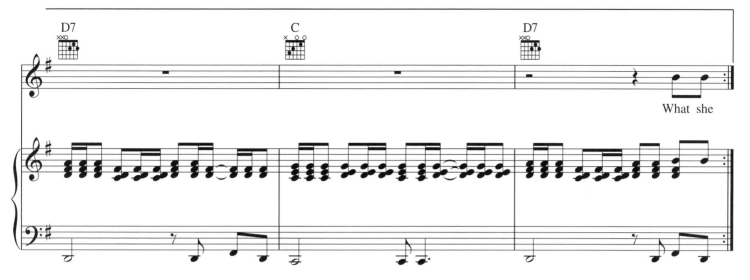

What she

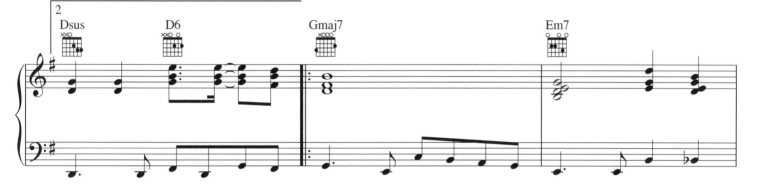

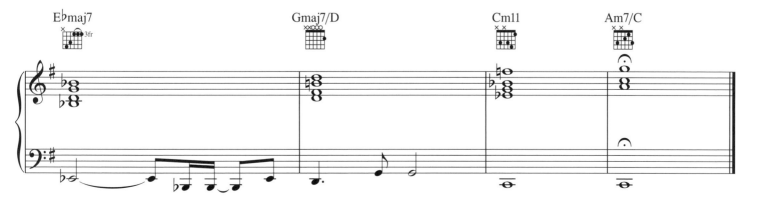

HOW SOON IS NOW

Words and Music by JOHNNY MARR
and STEVEN MORRISSEY

Moderately fast

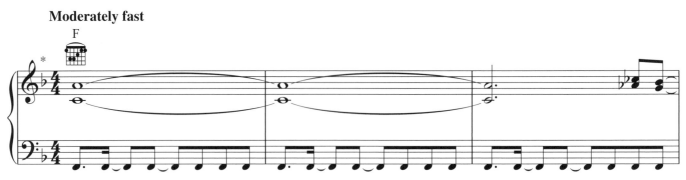

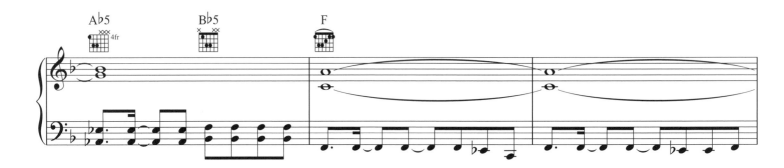

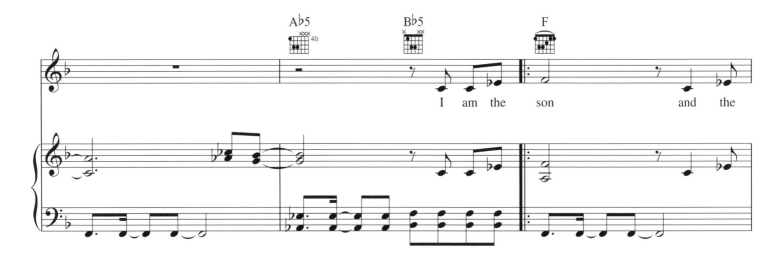

I am the son and the

heir

of a shy - ness that is crim-i-nal-ly vul-

Originally recorded a half step higher.

gar. I am the son and heir ___ of noth-ing ___ in par-ti-cu-lar.

You shut your mouth, _ how can you say ___

___ I go a-bout things the wrong _ way? I am hu - man and I need to be loved, _

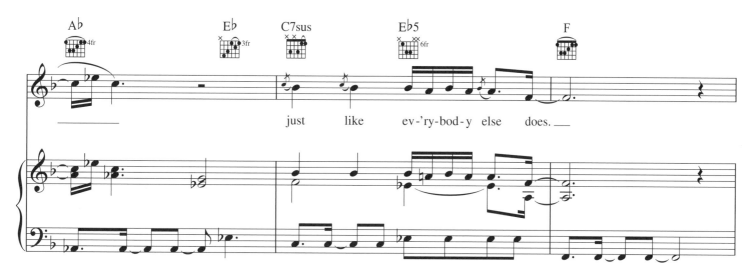

just like ev-'ry-bod-y else does. ___

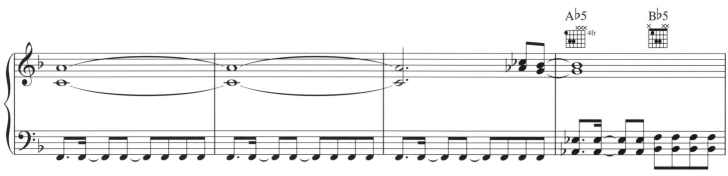

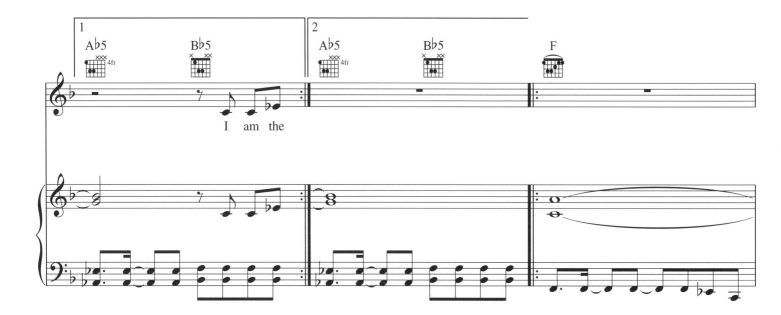

I am the

There's a club if you'd like to go. _____ You could meet some-bod-y _____ who real-ly loves _

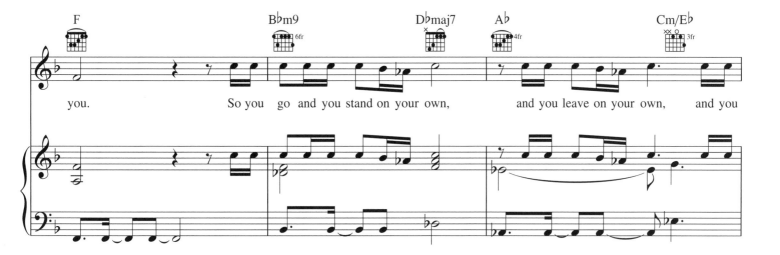

you. So you go and you stand on your own, and you leave on your own, and you

go home and you cry and you want to die. ___

Repeat and Fade

LAST NIGHT I DREAMT THAT SOMEBODY LOVED ME

Words and Music by JOHNNY MARR
and STEVEN MORRISSEY

Dark and driving

Last night I dreamt

that some-bod-y loved me.

No hope, no harm; just an-oth-er false a-larm.

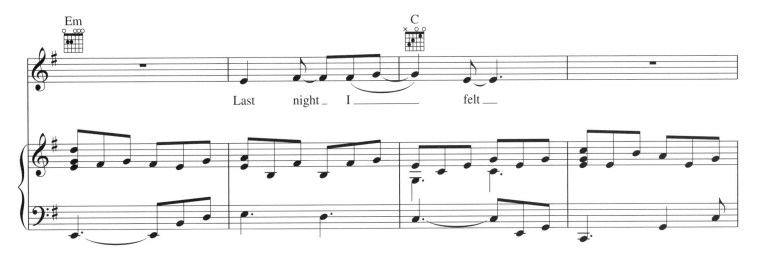

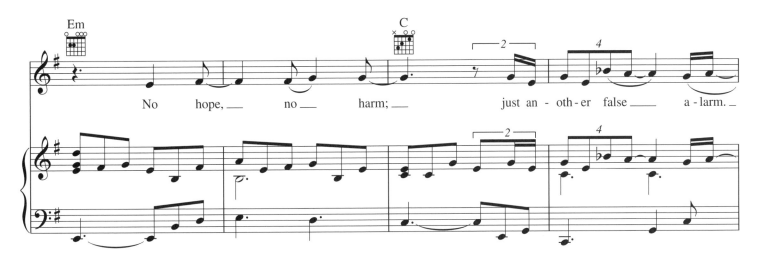

So tell me, how__ long__

be - fore_____ the last_____ one?__

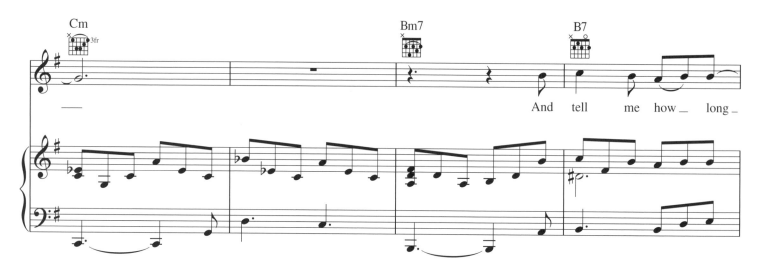

And tell me how__ long__

be - fore_____ the right_____ one?__

The sto - ry is old, ___

I ___ know, ___ but it goes ___ on. ___

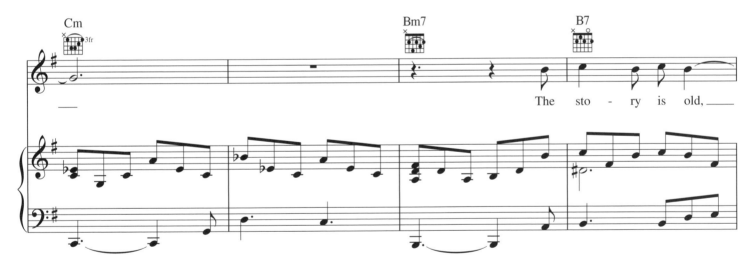

The sto - ry is old, ___

I ___ know, ___ but it goes ___ on. ___

PLEASE, PLEASE, PLEASE, LET ME GET WHAT I WANT

Words and Music by JOHNNY MARR
and STEVEN MORRISSEY

Acoustic Rock, with a strum

Good times, _____ for a change. ___

See, the luck I've had _____ can make a good man turn bad. _

So please, please,

please, _____ let me, ____ let me, ___ let me, _____ let me __

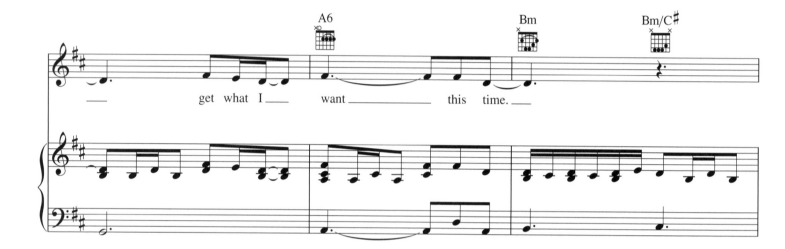

__ get what I ___ want _____ this time. ___

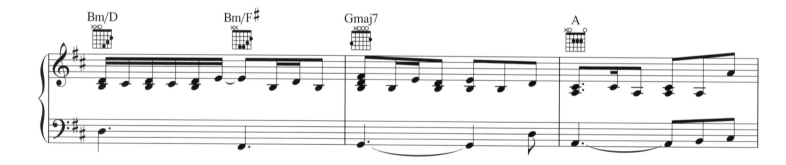

Have - n't had a dream ____ in a long ___ time. _

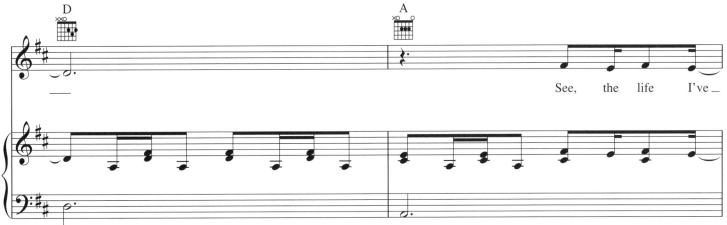

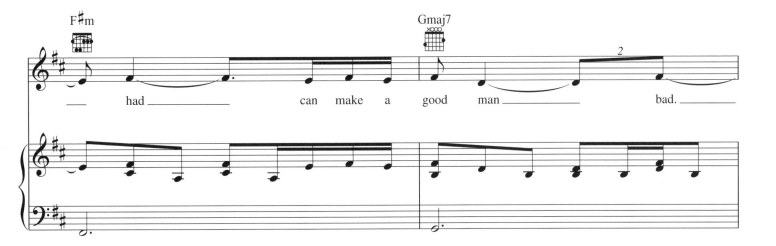

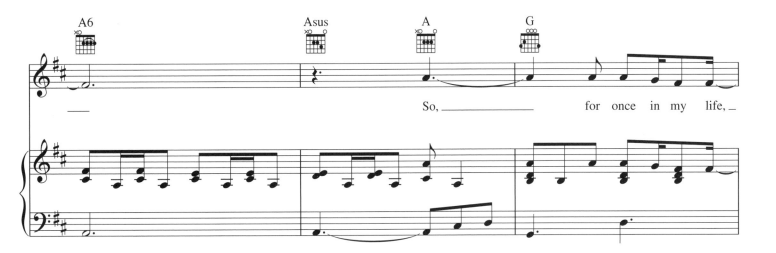

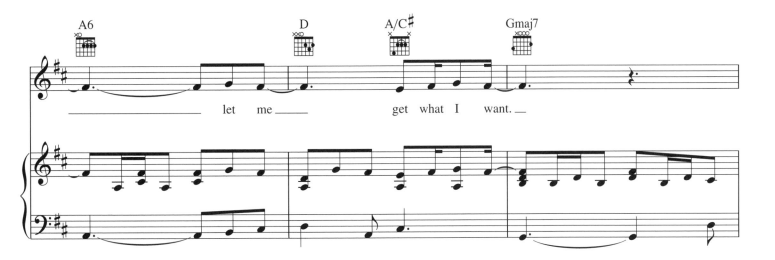

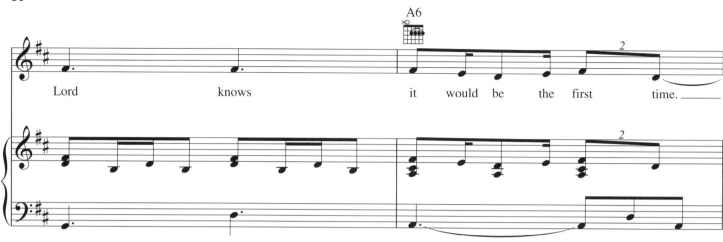

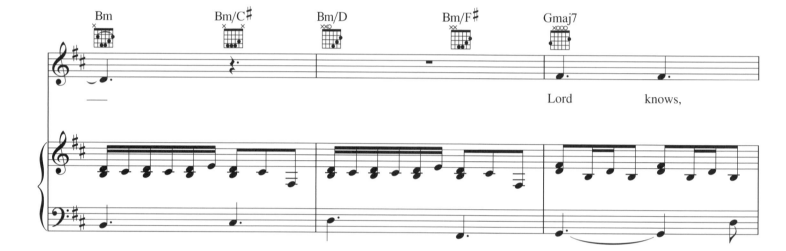

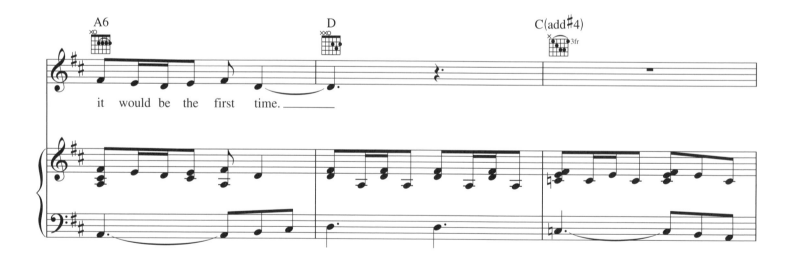

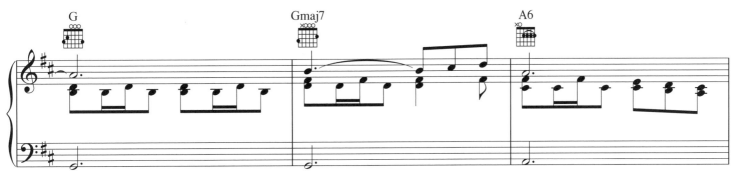

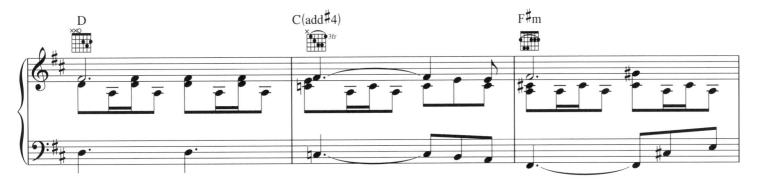

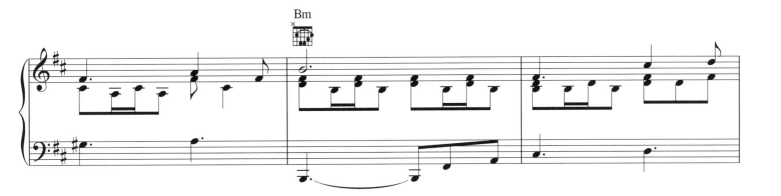

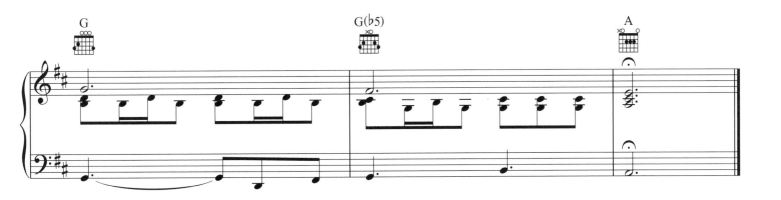

THERE IS A LIGHT THAT NEVER GOES OUT

Words and Music by JOHNNY MARR
and STEVEN MORRISSEY

Medium Rock

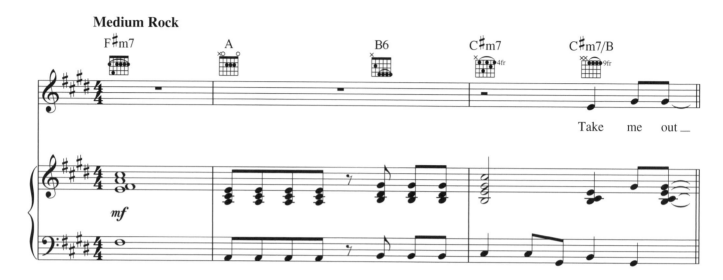

Take me out

to - night, where there's

mu - sic and there's peo - ple, and they're young and a - live.

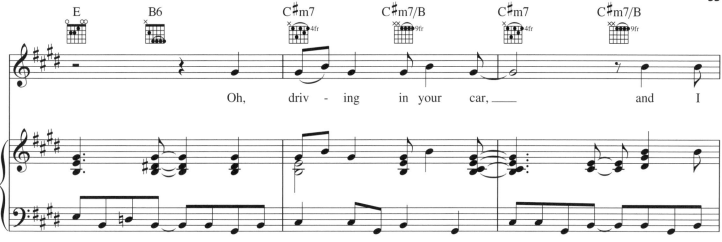

Oh, driv-ing in your car, ___ and I

nev-er, nev-er want to go home, __ be-cause I have-n't got one

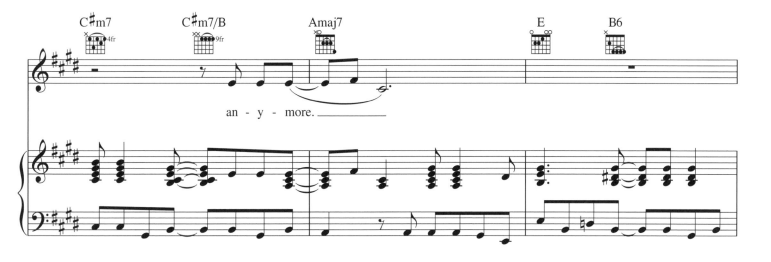

an - y - more. ___

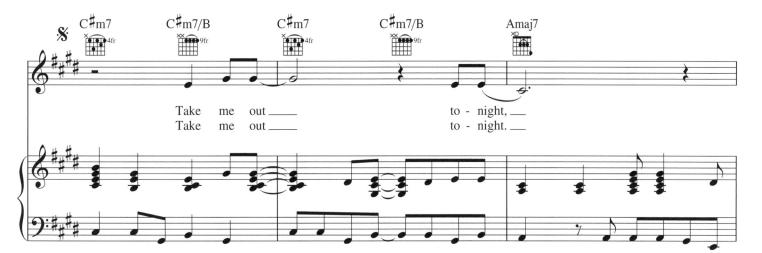

Take me out ___ to - night, __
Take me out ___ to - night. __

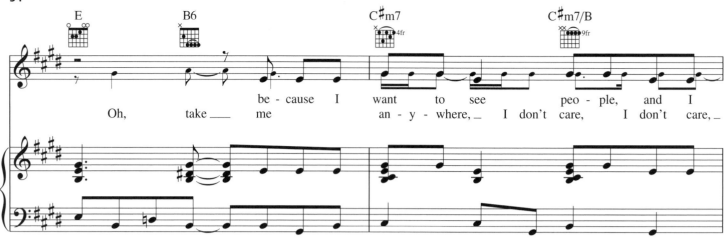

be - cause I want to see peo - ple, and I
Oh, take ___ me an - y - where, ___ I don't care, I don't care, ___

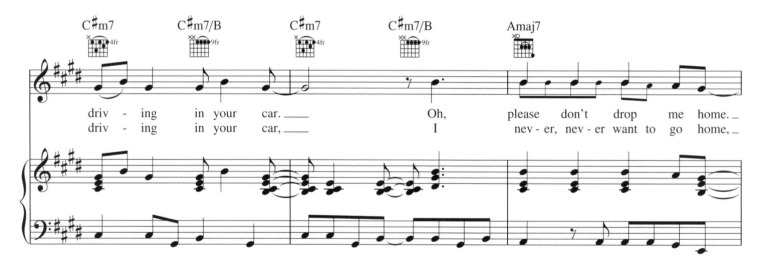

want to see life. _____
___ I don't care. _____ Oh,
Oh,

driv - ing in your car. ___ Oh, please don't drop me home. ___
driv - ing in your car, ___ I nev - er, nev - er want to go home, ___

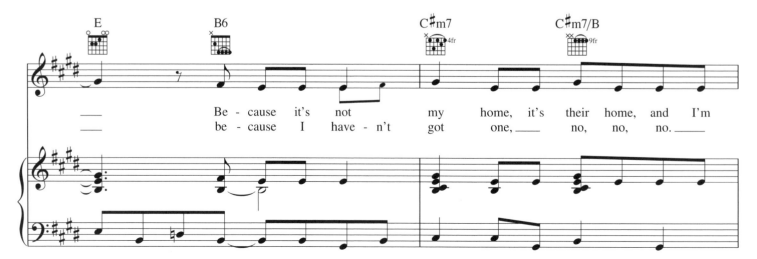

Be - cause it's not my home, it's their home, and I'm
be - cause I have - n't got one, ___ no, no, no. ___

wel-come no more. ___
Oh, I have-n't got one.
Oh, ___

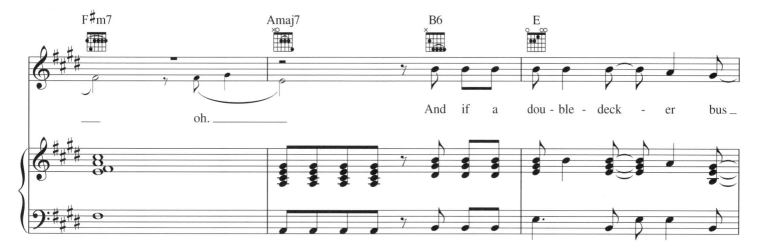

___ oh. ___
And if a dou-ble-deck - er bus ___

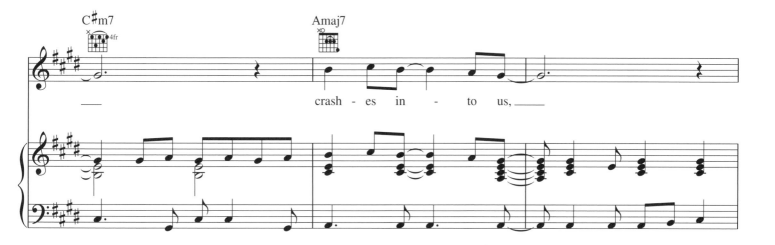

___ crash - es in - to us, ___

to die ___ by your ___ side ___ is such a heav-en-ly way ___ to die. ___

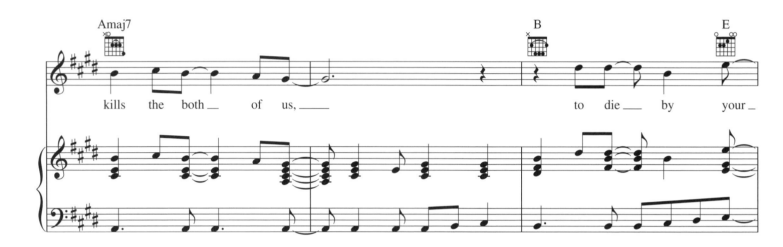

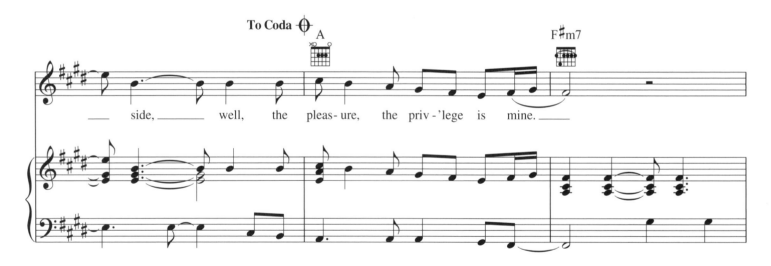

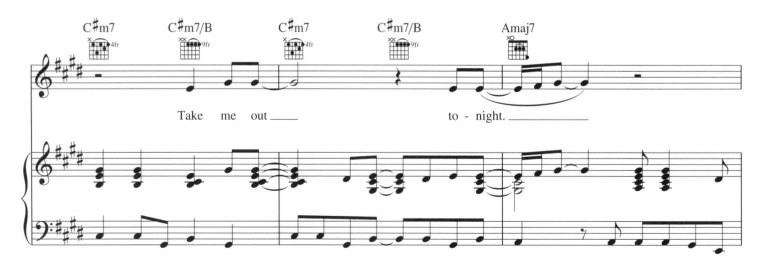

Take ___ me an-y-where, ___ I don't care, I don't ___ care, ___

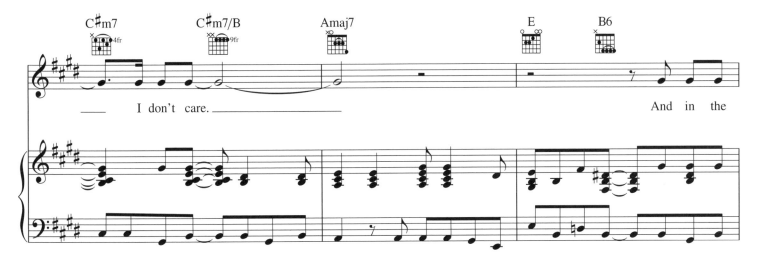

___ I don't care. _____ And in the

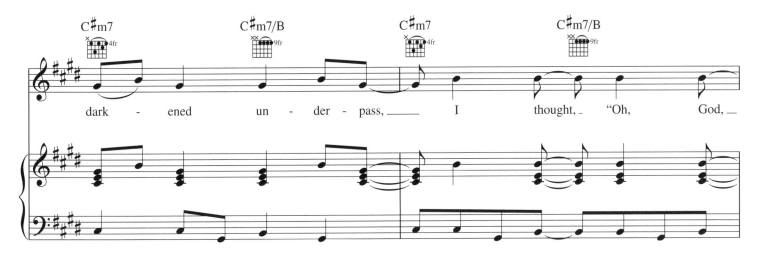

dark - ened un-der-pass, _____ I thought, _ "Oh, God, _

___ my chance has come at last." _____ But then a

58

strange fear gripped me, and I just could-n't ask. _____

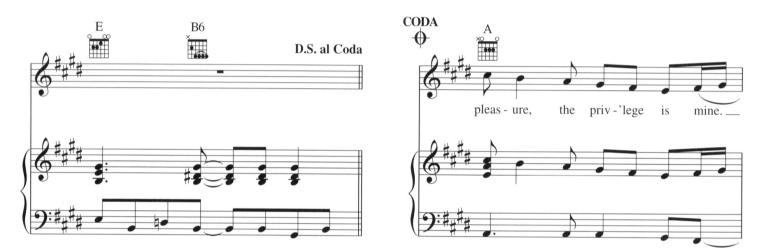

D.S. al Coda

CODA

pleas - ure, the priv-'lege is mine. __

__ Oh, there __ is a light and it nev - er goes out. __

Vocal ad lib. and fade on repeat

There is a light that nev - er goes out. __ There is a light that

never goes out. ___ There is a light and it nev-er goes out. ___

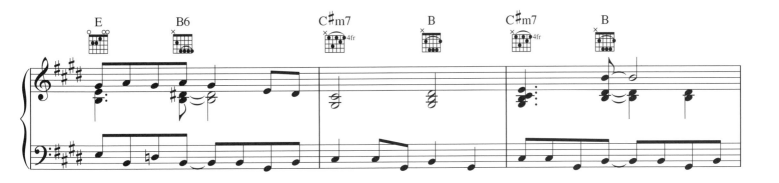

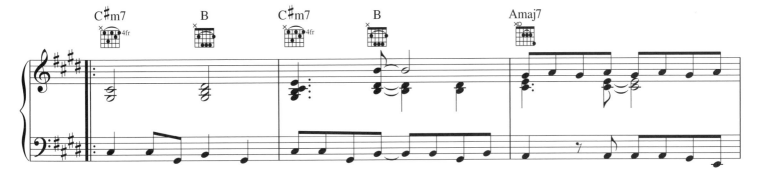

WHAT DIFFERENCE DOES IT MAKE?

Words and Music by JOHNNY MARR
and STEVEN MORRISSEY

Brisk Rock

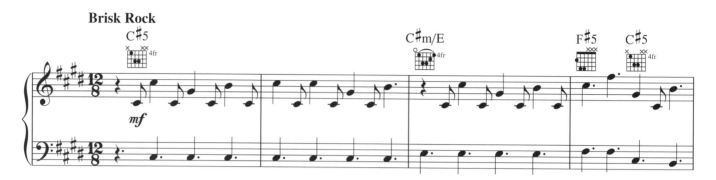

All __ men __ have __ se - crets, and here __ is __ mine,
The __ dev - il __ will __ find __ work __ for __ i -
Oh, __ the dev - il __ will __ find __ work __ for __ i -

_____ so let it be known. ___
- dle hands __ to do. ___
- dle hands __ to do. ___

For we have been through hell __
I stole _____ and I
I stole and then I lied __

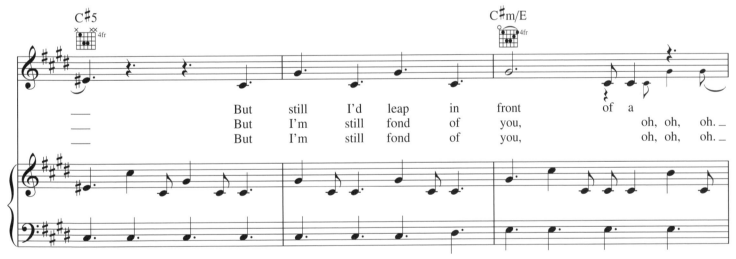

day. But I'm still fond of you, _____ oh, oh, oh. _

Oh, _____
Lead vocal ad lib.

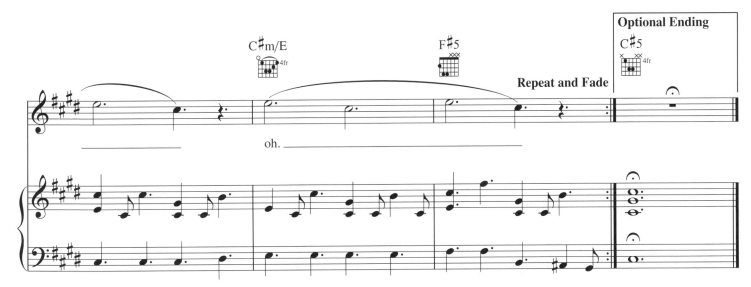

Repeat and Fade

Optional Ending

_____ oh. _____

THIS CHARMING MAN

Words and Music by JOHNNY MARR
and STEVEN MORRISSEY

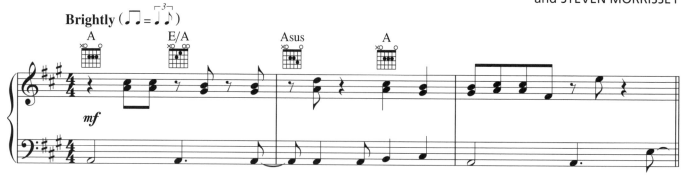

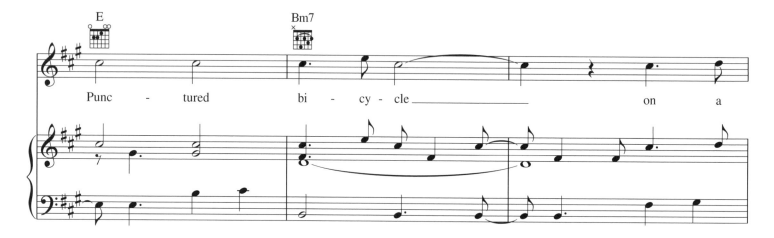

Punc - tured bi - cy - cle _____ on a

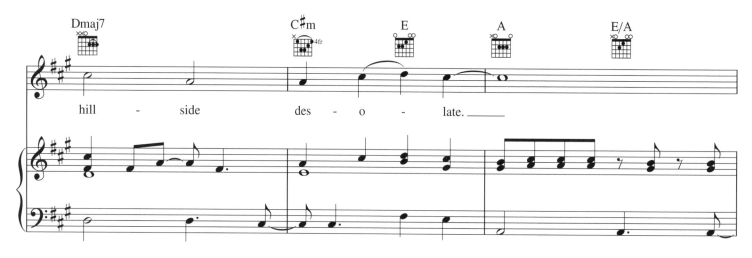

hill - side des - o - late. _____

Will na - ture make a man of ___ me ___

yet,

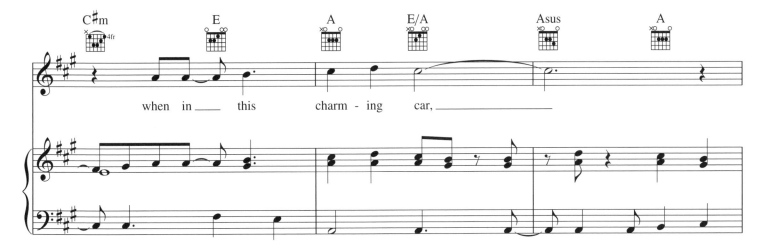

when in ___ this charm - ing car, _____

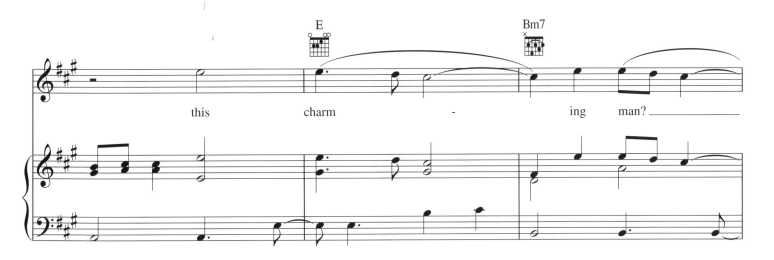

this charm - ing man? _____

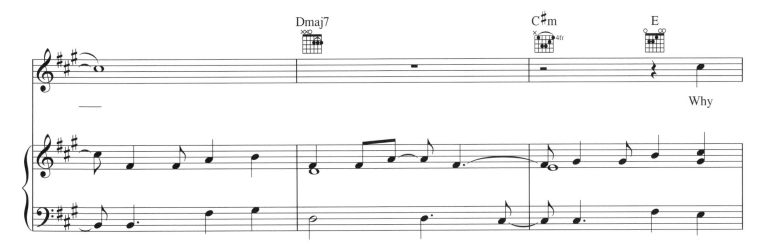

Why

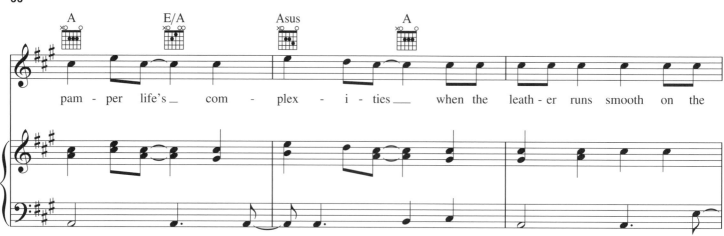

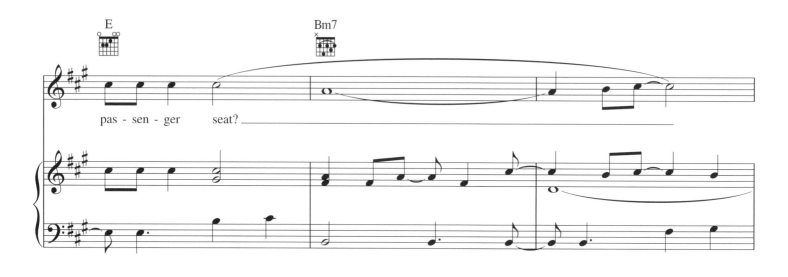

This man said, "It's grue - some that

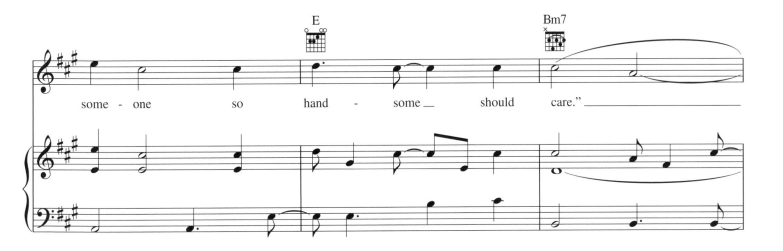

some - one so hand - some should care."

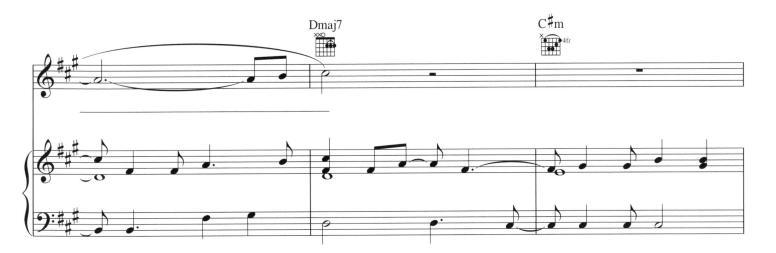

68

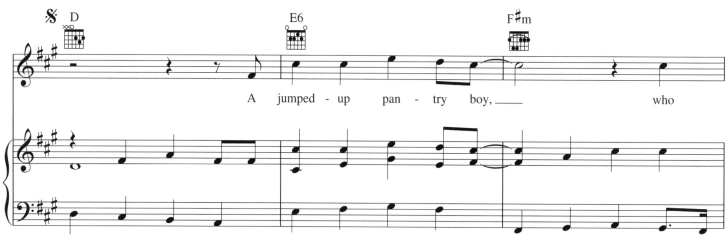

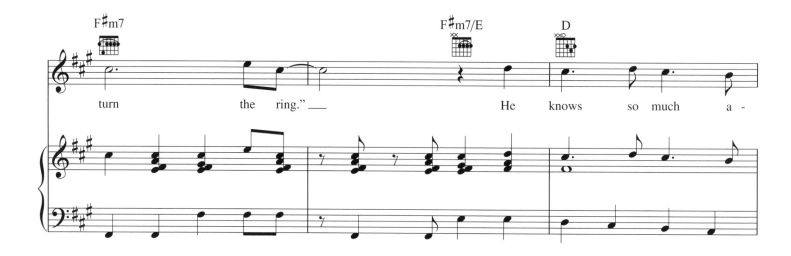

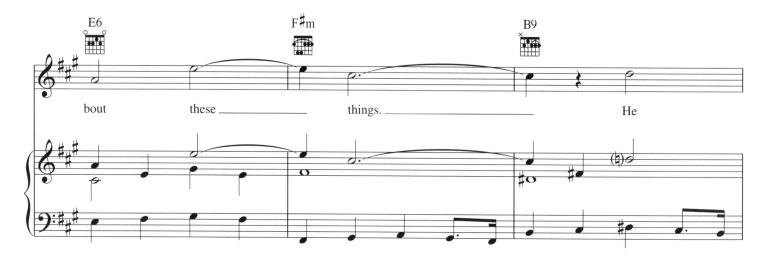

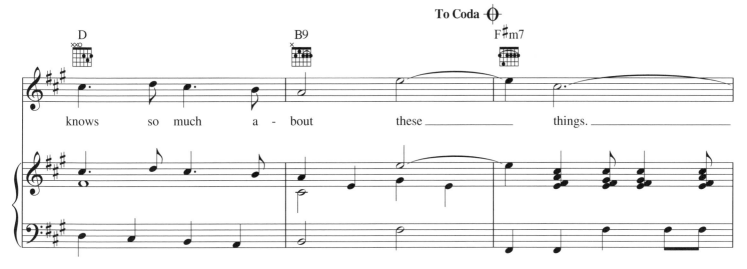

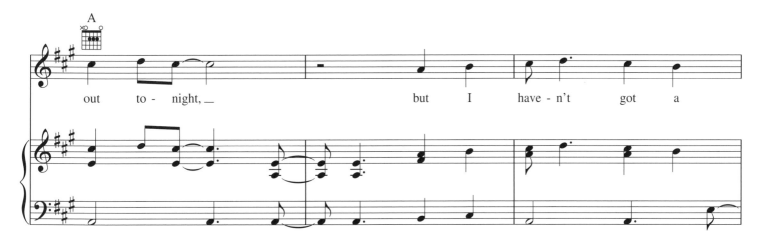

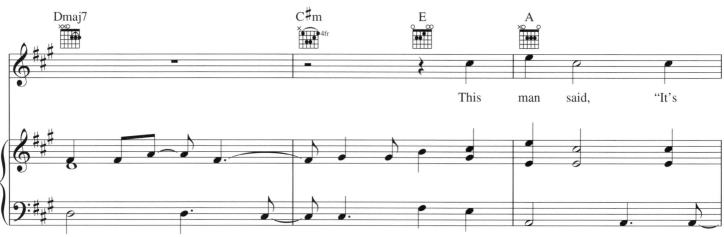

This man said, "It's

grue - some that some - one so hand - some __ should

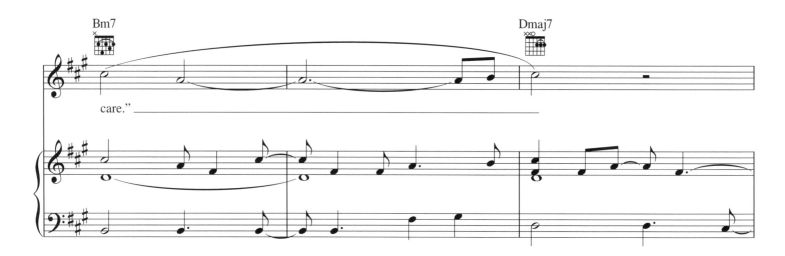

care." _____

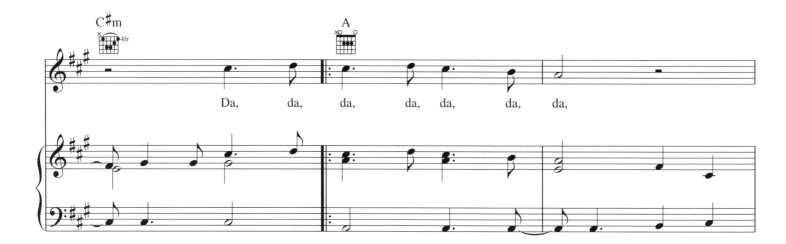

Da, da, da, da, da, da, da,

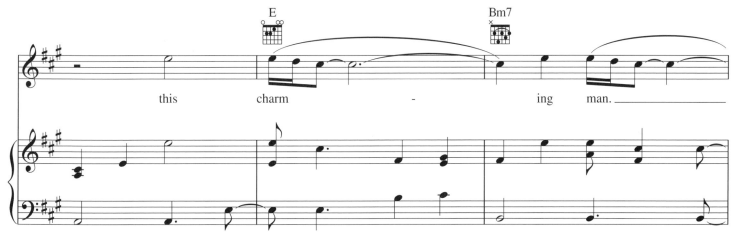

this charm - ing man. _____

1
Da, _____ da,

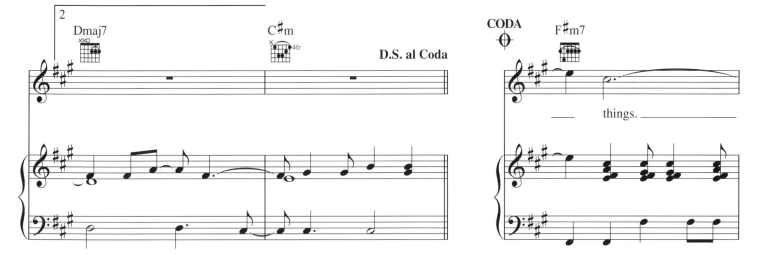

2

D.S. al Coda

CODA

_____ things. _____

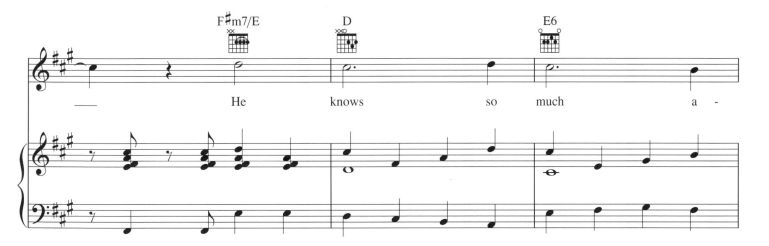

He knows so much a-

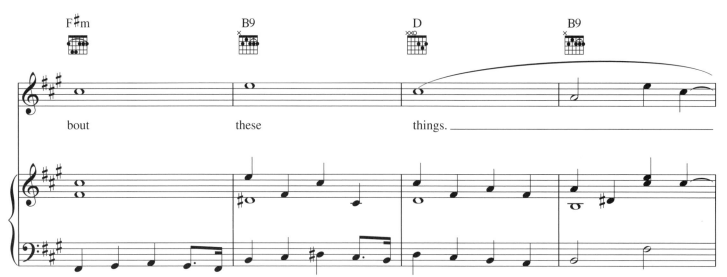

bout   these   things.

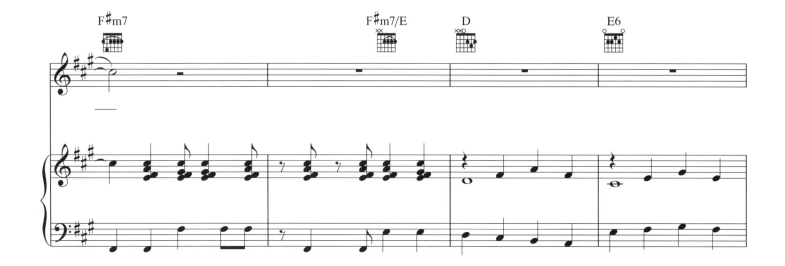

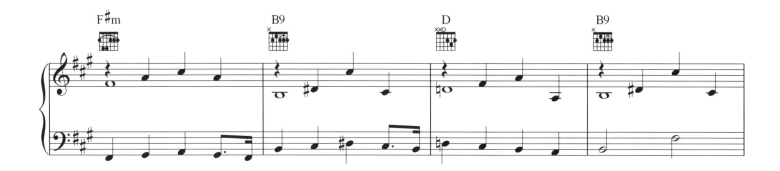